PICK UP SOME BALLS

A BEGINNER'S GUIDE TO JUGGLING BALLS, CLUBS AND RINGS

British Library Cataloguing-in-Publication Data
A catalogue record for this book is available from the
British Library

CONTENTS

Introduction to
Indian Clubs

'Indian clubs', or 'Iranian clubs' belong to a category of exercise equipment used for developing strength, and in juggling. In appearance, they resemble elongated bowling-pins, and are commonly made out of wood. They come in all shapes and sizes however, ranging from a few pounds each, to fifty pounds, and are commonly swung in certain patterns as part of exercise programs. They were often used in class formats, predominantly in Iran, where members would perform choreographed routines, led by an instructor; remarkably similar to modern aerobics classes. Despite their name, 'Indian clubs' actually originated in ancient Persia, Egypt and the Middle East, where they were used by wrestlers. The practice has continued to the present day, notably in the varzesh-e bastani tradition practiced in the zurkaneh of Iran. British colonialists first came across these eastern artefacts in India however, hence the name. The 'Indian clubs' became exceedingly popular back in the UK, especially during the health craze of the Victorian era. In a book written in 1866, by an American sports enthusiast, S.D. Kehoe, it was stated that 'as a means of physical culture, the Indian Clubs stand pre-eminent among the varied apparatus of Gymnastics now in use.' He had visited England in 1861, and was so impressed with the sport that he began to manufacture and sell clubs to the American public in 1862. They were used by military cadets and upper class ladies alike, and even appeared as a gymnastic event at the 1904 and 1932 Olympics. Their popularity began to wane in the 1920s however, with the growing predilection for organised sports. The modern juggling club was inspired by the 'Indian club' though; first repurposed for juggling by DeWitt Cook in the 1800s. He taught his step son, Claude Bartram to juggle with them, who later went on to form the first 'club juggling act'. Today, their popularity has been revived somewhat, by fitness enthusiasts who that they are a far safer means of excising, rather than the traditional 'free weight regimens'. Nostalgic replicas of the original clubs are still manufactured, as well as modern engineering updates to the concept, such as the Clubbell.

JUGGLING WITH BALLS

Games with balls have been popular since ancient times. In those days, such sports formed an important part of the exercise of every age group. Greeks and Romans had their own playing courts and fields, and youngsters practised hitting, throwing, and catching much as boys do today. In every age, the round ball has had an irresistible appeal: people toss and catch it, hit it, and push it with their hands, feet, and even with their heads! Children stand in front of house walls and never seem to tire of throwing a ball back and forth. Many of us have perhaps made a ball bounce on a toe. And in playing soccer, as everyone knows, you must be able to control the ball with your head.

The word "ball" comes from French, and the basic meaning of the French word *bal* is *dance*. Looking further back into linguistic history, we find the Latin word *ballare* meaning *to dance*.

The goal is literally to "teach the balls to dance." With skill, the balls should dance and circle around, up and down, back and forth, defying gravity with their flight. First, get yourself five or six balls of the same size but with as different coloration as possible. Important: these should be no larger than tennis balls. In the beginning, in fact, you should use balls that are even smaller than tennis balls. Give special attention, also, to the *surface* quality of the balls you use. The character of the surface is very important in juggling. Neither highly polished nor fuzzy tennis balls should be used. Highly polished balls become moist from unavoidable perspiration on your hands and slip too easily when they are grasped. Fuzzy balls absorb moisture and make the palms of your hands too dry for a firm grip. Balls with rough and unvarnished surfaces are your best choice, and in some cases, even solid rubber balls can be used.

When you have acquired balls of the right size, your juggling can begin. Looked at from an artistic standpoint, ball juggling presents an impressive exhibition of tossing and catching. Your skilled hand directs the movement of the balls, as you use your knowledge of gravity. We will often speak of gravity in this book, but fear not, you won't have to study the laws of physics! As a beginning juggler, however, you should understand some of the physical forces with which you will be dealing later on.

Obviously, in learning the art of juggling, you will begin with easy tricks and gradually go on to more difficult tricks. It is important, therefore, to read the beginning chapter on juggling carefully, and work through the exercises until you have mastered them. The illustrations will help explain proper hand motions. Let's begin with two balls.

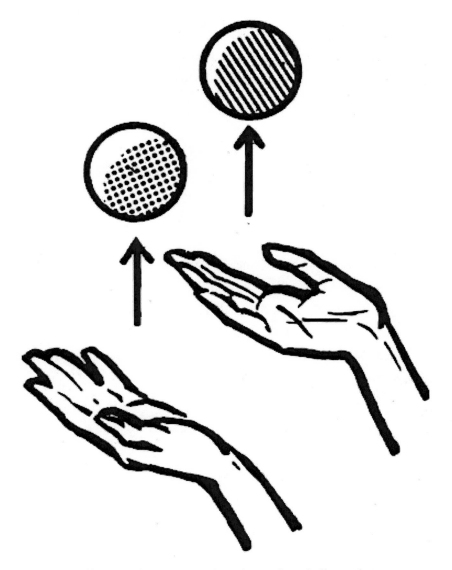

Fig. 1. Alternate the tossing and catching of two balls until you can do this easily. Then try tossing higher.

1. TWO BALLS

Limber up your hands and fingers with some warming-up exercises. If you have ever looked behind the scenes of a circus performance, you have watched the energy and care with which performers limber up their bodies, warm up, and practise their act. Such exercises must precede any "star" performance. So you, too, will have to limber up your stiff fingers.

Next, take the two balls, one in each hand, and throw both up in front of you at the same time and catch them again. Try high and low tosses, making sure that one ball goes just as high as the other. You will soon see that one hand tends to throw higher than the other, depending on whether you are right- or left-handed. During these tosses, notice which hand is stronger and adjust your throw accordingly. Your aim is to have both hands working equally hard (Fig. 1).

For a second exercise, throw the balls crosswise from hand to hand (Fig. 2). You can avoid collisions in mid-air if one ball has a head start or is thrown higher than the other. It is by no means simple to make a perfect cross-throw. You should, therefore, practise it often. At the same time, your eye will learn quick co-ordination.

After these first two exercises, you can begin juggling two balls in a simple circular path. Hold a ball in each hand. Now throw one ball into the air so that it flies in a gentle arc over to the other hand. After a moment—while the ball is in flight—transfer the second ball into the hand which has just become free. This exchange motion should take place in a short horizontal direction.

In the meantime, keep your eye on the ball which is flying through the air. The horizontal exchange of the ball from one hand to the other is guided by a sense of touch which is not at all difficult to develop. You will learn this exercise with two balls quickly, but you have to practise it often to learn fluent tossing and catching motions. Naturally, you should practise tossing from left to right, as well as from right to left. Fig. 3 shows the motion from right to left.

Fig. 2. Your cross-throw should be smooth and steady.

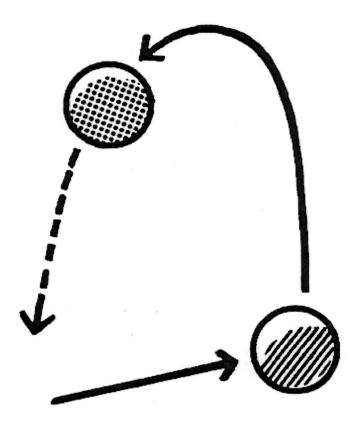

Fig. 3. Co-ordination and good timing are needed to juggle two balls in a circle.

At the beginning, you should practise faithfully, for not less than 15 minutes a day. Soon, juggling will be fun and the little balls will have an almost magnetic fascination for you.

Before long, you will be ready to begin juggling with two balls in *one* hand. To do this, hold both balls comfortably in the same hand with one ball in the palm of your hand

and the other farther forward on your fingers. The balls will touch lightly. First, try to throw the front ball up and catch it without letting the second ball interfere.

This is easy enough to do. Now it is time to throw the balls up and catch them again, in turn. Toss the first ball up. Before it can fall back into your hand, toss up the second ball. Hop—hop—hop! The balls will dance up and down in the same hand, one after the other. It is great fun when you have the hang of it. If the balls collide in the air, slip out of your hand, or drop to the ground, the beginning juggler simply has to recall the proverb "practice makes perfect." Just pick up the balls and try your skill again. To avoid bending frequently to retrieve balls, stand in front of a sofa while you practise. Then you have only half as far to bend and can pick up the fallen balls more quickly!

It is a matter of individual preference whether to make the balls fly by each other sidewise or have them make a slight circle. Try both methods. Also try to increase your speed by juggling with very low throws. This way, your hand will become more skilful in catching and tossing. Fig. 4 shows how the balls should dance up and down in one hand.

You should not forget to practise one-handed juggling with both your left and right hands. In later exercises this will be very useful. The master juggler cannot permit himself to be "one-sided," that is, to be a left- or right-handed person. So be sure you give both hands equal practice.

After juggling with two balls in one hand, proceed to further tossing and catching exercises. For example, practise the following ball toss, which you can then demonstrate in front of a group of your friends. It is always good for laughs.

Stand with your legs apart, take a ball, and bend forward. Then throw the ball between your legs as straight up as possible. Straighten up again very quickly and catch the ball. This will look like a very simple trick, to your friends. Then offer them the ball to try their skill. Now the fun begins! Everyone will be surprised where the balls land, when they are thrown back between the legs. Jokingly, point out to your guests the cost of breakage. Try this away from windows and breakables, of course! The starting position for this trick is shown in Fig. 5.

Here is another tossing motion which you should learn. This involves throwing a ball with one hand in an easy curve over your shoulder, then catching it with the other hand. After you catch the ball, toss it back again. Practise this by throwing alternately with your left and right hands.

The next step is to bounce a ball lightly off your forehead. A slight push with your forehead will increase the rebound. Then catch the ball. Try bouncing the ball on your forehead several times, before you catch it. After you have practised this, you can vary the trick by throwing the ball from under your raised knee.

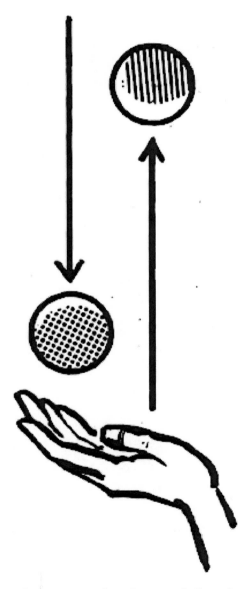

Fig. 4. (Right) Tossing and catching two balls with one hand.

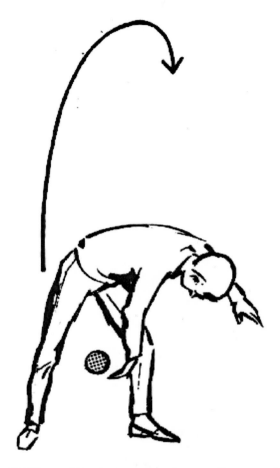

Fig. 5. (Left) Whoops! Be sure you straighten up fast enough to catch the ball. Then start all over again!

As soon as you are adept with two balls, you can add embellishments. For example, while two balls move up and down, let one of them bounce off your forehead and catch it. This double tossing can continue without interruption! You can also toss a ball from under a raised knee without stopping the motion of another ball. These exercises are useful because they involve your whole body in the business of juggling. You learn to react quickly, and can later strengthen your arm and hand movements.

A story is told about the master juggler, Enrico Rastelli, who attempted to perform a somersault in the air, while juggling. His untimely death, unfortunately, prevented a performance of this feat from ever reaching the public. We certainly do not expect to go this far, but various body motions are helpful while juggling.

After you have learned to toss and catch two balls well, you can go on to more difficult juggling exercises. The next step is to add a third ball. In the following sections, the number of balls used will be increased gradually and how far you can go towards perfecting your skill will depend on your individual effort.

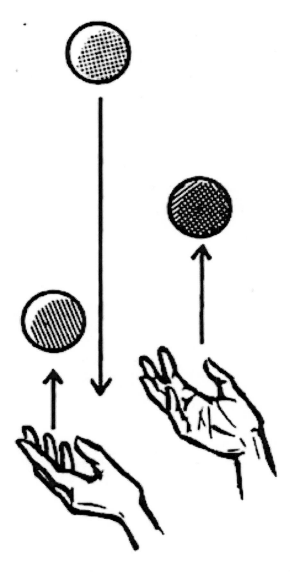

Fig. 6. Now the fun begins! The trick here is to keep one ball in the air all the time.

2. THREE BALLS

This is where real juggling begins. Anyone who has practised well with two balls can master three quickly.

First, take two balls in one hand and hold a third in the other. Then let each hand toss and catch by itself or shift to crossover tosses. Do the easier exercises first. Start by throwing two balls up and down with one hand, as you have already learned. Keep the third ball, for the present, in your other hand. Whenever it seems appropriate, try to throw the third ball up and down in the same rhythm. Thus, while you are juggling two balls in your right hand, you are tossing a third with your left. An observer can see two balls go up together, then one, then two, then one . . . The single ball dancing between the other two makes a pretty picture (Fig. 6). You can master this exercise quickly and then go on to the next step: the crossover toss with three balls. This is lots of fun, and with it you enter the realm of real juggling.

Take two balls in one hand and a third ball in the other. Your first ball must fly from the hand holding two. Where do you throw it? Into your other hand, of course. How? In an easy curve, about a yard high. Now toss the third ball (the extra one) from one hand to the other a few times, catching it carefully while still holding the other two balls. You will probably feel the urge to toss off the ball you have been holding, so that your hand can be free for the catch. This brings you to juggling three balls. For the point is not simply to throw one ball back and forth, but to get three balls into flight. This takes place in the following easy order: 1, 2, 3; 1, 2, 3.

Throw ball 1 (the extra ball in one hand) first. A second later—before ball 1 reaches your other hand—toss out ball 2 from that hand, freeing the hand to catch ball 1. A second later, toss ball 3, freeing that hand to catch ball 2.

The balls, tossed out alternately from each hand split seconds after they are caught, are constantly in motion, with one ball always in the air.

Your tosses should follow a smooth, definite rhythm. In this way, the balls will arrive in your hands and be ready for retossing, like clockwork. Fig. 7 shows an instant in the paths of flight. Ball 1 was thrown first, and has most of its path behind it. It will be caught by the left hand in a moment. Ball 2 has just been thrown from the left hand and is near the high point of its flight path, from where it will begin to drop into the right hand. Ball 3 will follow the same path as ball 1. Study the drawing carefully; it explains the directions pictorially.

You will have taken your first steps forward in juggling when you can catch one or two of the three balls tossed. Do not let it worry you if the third ball drops to the floor. With persistent practice, you will soon be able to toss—and catch—all three balls. The more often the balls fall to the ground, the more conscientiously you must practice. Remember, no effort—no reward! This proverb applies to every juggler.

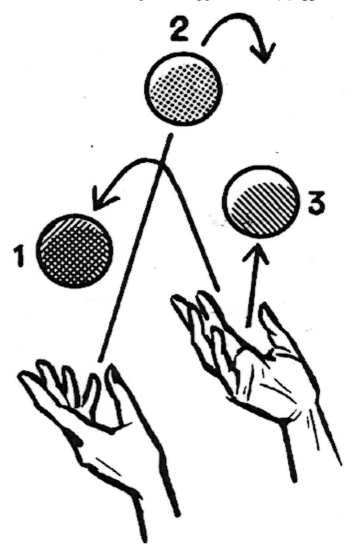

Fig. 7. One, two, three—one, two, three. Not quite as easy as

counting, but with a little practice, you'll get the knack.

Once you can handle three balls successfully, you will experience your first real thrill as a juggler. You can now show off your skill to friends and relatives. How fascinated they will be, watching you juggle red, green, and blue balls from hand to hand! Remember, too, that it is hard to count three juggled balls while they are moving. There seems to be more than three balls! Naturally, your audience will want to try juggling too. Explain how it is done, and then watch as ball after ball drops to the floor. No one will be able to match your skill, without having practised!

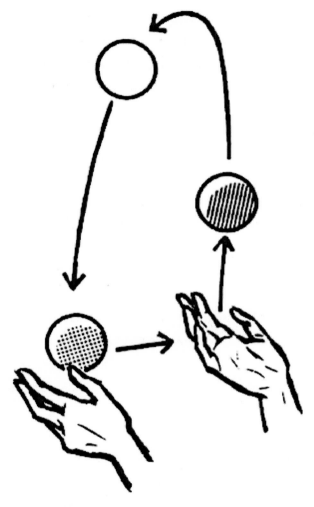

Fig. 8. Keep the balls moving steadily, just the way you see it here: over—up—around and down.

Now that you have mastered the use of three balls, you are ready to learn other juggling tricks, using them. First, make the three balls move through the air in a circle. Fig. 8 shows their path. As you can see, they are no longer thrown crosswise. In the picture, it is always the *right* hand which tosses the balls up. The left hand catches them and passes them over to the right.

The game begins by throwing the first ball from one hand. A second ball is quickly thrown from the same hand and this hand is now free to catch the third ball (thrown with the other hand) and toss it after the first two. Of course, your hand movements in this trick must be quicker than when you threw crosswise. With a little effort you can soon master this "circle-around" game. Be sure you practise it towards the right as well as the left. You can carry it out with either low or high tosses. The lower you let the balls circle, the faster your hands must work. Later, when you are more skilful, you can change from crosswise to circular juggling, without stopping. For the time being, however, study the "circle-around" game carefully as shown in Fig. 8.

Here is a variation you can try, when you have practised the circle game thoroughly. Juggle three balls in a circle, with one arm stretched upwards. In this position, the arriving balls can be caught with an easy hand motion and directed diagonally over the ball of your thumb towards the hand below. Here they are caught and sent right back up again. The effect is very amusing when you can hold your extended hand up almost without motion.

Fig. 9. Here's how it's done—notice the position of the arms.

In the middle of this act, you can add one more trick. Catch and hold all three balls in your extended hand. While the three balls are in your upper hand, continue the throwing motion of your lower hand (as if the act were still going on). Pretend not to notice that you are throwing "empty" and that the three balls are stuck above. "Wake up" only when your audience begins to laugh. Look up in surprise, and coax the three balls down for continued play. Let them drop, one after another, and your act can go on. Fig. 9 shows the position of the arms, and the paths of the balls.

Now look for further variations. A good juggler should be as versatile as possible. Here are other exercises you can try:

(a) Walk back and forth while juggling.

(b) Stand on a chair while juggling, and jump down without losing the balls.

(c) Approach a wall while juggling the three balls and let them strike it in the middle of the game. (You'll have to practise this one often!)

(d) Let one ball bounce on the floor, bend over a little, and bring it back into play.

(e) Let one ball fall on your toe, then kick it back up into play. (This works best with large balls!)

While juggling crosswise:

(f) Let a ball bounce off your forehead.

(g) Throw single balls from under your raised knees—left and right alternately.

(h) Throw one ball quickly forward from behind your back.

(i) Sit down on the floor and get up again, without interrupting the game.

(j) Let the backs of your hands strike a table surface lightly so that the beating rhythm can be heard.

(k) Use three balls of different sizes.

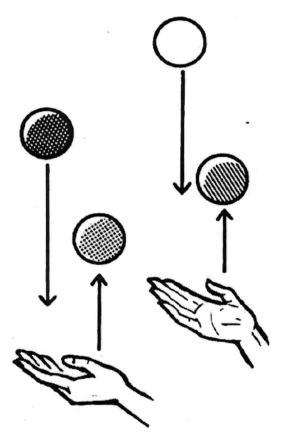

Fig. 10. Tossing two balls with each hand is not as hard as it looks. Start with one hand first. Then, when you are ready, juggle with both hands (either alternately or at the same time).

3. FOUR BALLS

After several weeks of practice, juggling three balls will have become easy and you can set yourself further goals. You will be happy to find that you have already learned, through the earlier exercises how to juggle four balls. How is that possible? Very simple! Each hand has mastered juggling with two balls. If you juggle at the same time with your right and left hands—which is not particularly difficult—then you have altogether, of course, four balls. So, without learning any new throwing and catching motions, you can already juggle four balls! There is no crossing over; the balls go straight up and down.

Now begin. Each hand holds two balls. It is up to you whether you throw right and left at the same time, or alternately. If you toss at the same time, you will have a matching double play of two balls each. It makes a more effective display, however, when the tossing and catching are done in turn. You will soon find that this is easy enough to do. If the balls collide once in a while and drop to the floor, try placing your hands farther apart, to give the balls more room. With four balls, also, you will want to throw high and low, to gain confidence. In giving a performance, use balls of four different hues, or two matched pairs of different hues (two red and two blue, for example), and let them rise and fall alternately (Fig. 10).

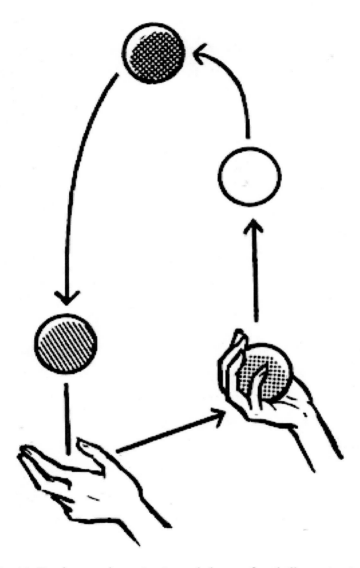

Fig. 11. Fast but steady tossing is needed to get four balls moving in a circular path.

Here is a more difficult trick, using four balls, which you can master with a little effort. It is juggling four balls around in a circle, and is exactly like the earlier juggling with three balls. One hand tosses up, the other catches and passes quickly across. If you can make three balls circle skilfully, you will succeed with four, as well. To start, hold two balls in each hand. Then toss up the two balls in your right hand (one after the other) as quickly as possible. The exchange from your left hand should begin immediately. The two balls in your left hand are passed over, one after the other, before the first tossed ball (from your right hand) drops into your left hand. This works best when the exchange begins as quickly as possible.

In Fig. 11, you can see the position of the four balls at one moment of the action. One ball after the other follows a circular path from the right hand to the left, is quickly caught, then sent with lightning speed over to the right hand again. When you master this exercise you can expect loud applause from your audience, for you will have reached an almost professional level of juggling.

Notice how high the juggler must toss, to keep five balls moving.

4. FIVE BALLS

For those who are ambitious enough to want to move on to exhibition accomplishments, juggling with five balls will now be described. Here, you ascend the heights of the professional juggler. It is a real accomplishment to make five balls dance up and down with seemingly weightless motion, and in regulated order. The amateur performer will realize, from his previous experience, that *order* rules in tossing and catching. Besides an exact knowledge of the path of flight, juggling with five balls also requires increased arm and hand speeds. But you have already developed your skill to where you can start practising this new assignment.

Begin by holding three balls in one hand and two in the other. Naturally, you toss first from the hand holding three balls. Immediately afterwards, a ball flies out of your other hand, then a ball from your first hand again, then another from the opposite hand, and finally, the fifth ball. Of course, you must toss very quickly! At first, just try getting the balls into the air. Toss them up, in order, as quickly as possible: right—left—right—left—right.

Now you are standing in the midst of tumbling balls! Collect them, and begin again. Your hands will soon become skilled enough to catch at least some of the balls. Try practising over a sofa, so that you can pick up the dropped balls quickly. And if a piece of furniture adds to your difficulties because you have to fish the balls out from underneath, place a board in front and your problem is solved!

After some success in tossing up the five balls, be satisfied if, at first, you manage to catch one or two of the thrown balls. Remember, nothing is easy in the beginning! If you become discouraged, think about the many hours that professional jugglers have to put in practising, day after day. In spite of many difficulties, they finally master the art.

Juggling with five balls is considered a thoroughly professional accomplishment. This crowning skill belongs only to the persistent amateur, who is determined to outdo himself. If you are willing to work, and practise regularly, you can master juggling with five balls. Practise outdoors, in a garden, if you can. This is even more fun. If you practise indoors, be sure you have enough room, for you must toss higher when using five balls.

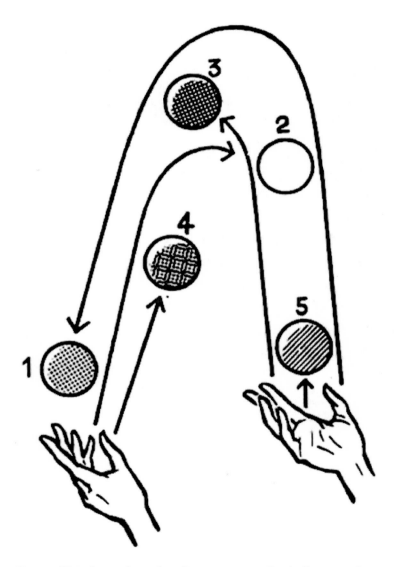

Fig. 12. This shows the order of tossing, using five balls. Try to keep the balls from colliding in air. If one drops, just pick it up and start again.

In Fig. 12, you see the throwing pattern with five balls. The order in which the balls rise can be seen from their numbers. Ball 1 is farthest in its flight path; ball 5 has just been thrown. The drawing shows nothing but the order of tossing: right—left—right—left—right. With the correct toss, there is always room for passing.

To an observer, juggling with five balls may look confusing at first. But a skilled juggler watches the order of flight as he tosses one ball after another, and takes pride in his perfect co-ordination and skill (see picture).

Your audience (whether relatives, friends, or casual observers) will realize how much skill is necessary for such a performance, and will not be stingy with their applause! And you, yourself, will appreciate all the more the remarkable accomplishment of those master jugglers you see in the circus, in variety shows, and at home on television.

Once you have learned to juggle five balls, you can consider a variation. By holding back two of the balls, you can switch from juggling five to juggling three. After a few rounds with three, start five balls juggling again. Do not try other variations, however, since juggling five balls demands your full attention and concentration.

5. SIX BALLS

If you want to increase your skill still further, and go on to join the juggling elite, you can try using six balls. Only a handful of jugglers in the entire world can juggle six or seven balls. Here, you are approaching a limit of the physical ability of man. Of course, the mathematical paths of flight of more ball tosses can be calculated and drawn, but carrying them out breaks down because of the impossibly fast hand-and-arm motions they require. Even with top skills, tossing and catching require split-second timing, which must be calculated. You have already seen that, in juggling five balls, extra time had to be provided, with a higher toss.

Juggling six balls is possible, with separate three-ball juggling in the left and right hands. (See section 7.)

If you have mastered one-handed triple juggling satisfactorily in the right as well as the left hand, you are ready to practise with six balls. The juggling can be started in unison: 2—2—2, toss up and catch. You can also (although it is considerably more difficult) toss and catch in syncopation. In any case, there is no tossing from one hand to the other, with six balls. Each hand holds three balls which are thrown up perpendicularly, in rapid succession.

6. SEVEN BALLS

Assume that you would like to become the juggler of the century and appear in all the great cities of the world, admired and applauded. You have nothing to do but practise with seven balls until these balls move through the air without accident. This, of course, requires enormous hand and body skills. Although we don't really expect that an uncrowned king waits among our readers, work with seven balls should at least be presented theoretically here.

Take four balls in one hand, and three in the other. The first problem appears immediately: how do you hold four balls in one hand? Well, it can be done using somewhat smaller balls. Three balls lie on your palm, and the fourth is set on top so that you can hold it by your finger tips. The second problem is tossing. It is not easy to throw seven balls up in smooth order! Also, your tossing speed must be increased tremendously in order to get all seven balls into play. The toss alternates from each hand, beginning with your right, and your cross-throw must begin with as flat a trajectory as possible. We won't go into catching the balls, here.

After looking over the last chapters, you will notice a definite pattern of throwing: juggling *uneven* numbers of balls calls for *crosswise* throws, and *even* numbers (two, four, or six balls) require a *vertical* toss and catch.

To wind up ball juggling, let us learn one final exercise. This will be one-handed juggling (which we practised in the beginning). But this time, we will be tossing and catching not two, but *three* balls in one hand.

Fig. 13. Careful timing, with speed, is needed to juggle three balls with one hand. Lower your hand, and toss higher (as necessary) to allow for the third ball.

7. THREE BALLS IN ONE HAND

To begin, hold three balls as comfortably as possible in one hand. Now toss them up quickly, one after the other. You must toss considerably faster than you did when tossing two balls, in the beginning. The three balls will collide often at first. The trick is that you have to find space for the flight of the third ball somewhere between the other two tossed balls. You can spread the toss out by moving your hand back and forth. This way, you can direct the third ball better. It is not as difficult as it seems; to make your task easier, toss higher. Be sure you practise where you have plenty of room height.

If the three balls dance too far apart, move in your free hand and switch over to two-handed juggling. You can go back to one-handed juggling whenever you wish. Fig. 13 shows one-handed juggling with three balls.

JUGGLING WITH RINGS

Many of us have seen the fine performances of jugglers working with bright, spinning rings. What a wonderful sight, to watch these rings moving up and down! No magic, no tricks—only the juggler's skill can send the rings up into the air, over and over again. Wouldn't you like to learn some of these skills, too?

You already have a basic foundation, from your juggling with balls. The same principles apply in juggling with rings. Some of you will even prefer ring juggling to ball juggling because rings show up better than balls at a distance. Also, you don't have to worry as much about collisions since the rings are narrow, and can fly past each other more easily. If they sometimes collide, they don't bounce away, as the balls do. Remember the law in physics: Every rotating body tends to maintain its motion. The spinning ring is like a gyroscope which tries to maintain its position and direction of flight.

The rings you use should measure about 8 to 12 inches in diameter. You can make your own rings by cutting them out of stiff cardboard, then covering them with brightly hued raffia or cloth. Gummed linen strips, which are very durable, can be bought in most stationery stores. Be careful not to cut the rings too narrow—they should be about 2 inches wide—

so that their surface has enough air resistance. Three rings of equal size are enough for a beginner, but if you wish, you can make more.

Because the height needed for ring juggling is greater than that for ball juggling, the ring juggler must always go outdoors when he wants to practise. Start by tossing and catching a single ring. The ring should spin evenly and not quiver. You will soon notice that tossing one ring gives you no particular trouble. Now take a second ring in your other hand and toss both rings up together. Then toss alternately—first left, then right.

Next, grasp *both* rings in *one* hand and practise tossing one ring without letting the second fall. Toss the first ring up using only your thumb and index finger. Use your other fingers to hold the second ring lightly. In less than an hour you will be able to juggle two rings with one hand. Practise this with the other hand, too, and then try high and low tosses to improve your skill in tossing and catching.

Soon, you will be ready to take a third ring in your hand. Follow the same principles you used for ball juggling and start tossing the rings crosswise. At first, it will take some effort to make a fine cross-throw with the rings. Be careful to throw high enough, so the rings will have room to cross. Fig. 14 shows juggling with two rings in one hand. After you are able to juggle two and three rings skilfully, you can try these variations:

(a) Juggling with one ring and one ball in one hand.

(b) Juggling with two balls and one ring.

(c) Juggling with one ball and two rings.

(d) Juggling with three rings, and occasionally tossing one under your knee or behind your back.

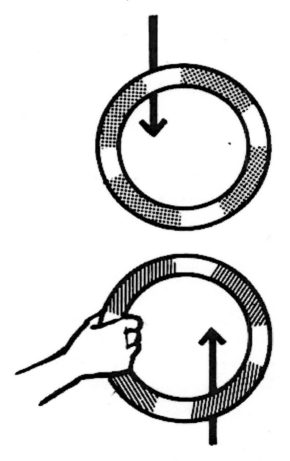

Fig. 14. Before tossing hold the ring with your thumb and index finger only, to release it easily.

(e) Tossing three rings in a circle. (This makes a fine display!)

(f) Throwing two rings up, left and right simultaneously, and letting a third dance up and down in the middle.

The resourceful amateur juggler will continually try out new exercises, and look for new variations beyond those suggested. In any case, be sure you practise juggling *combinations* of objects. It is thrilling to watch a ball and ring dance in the air *together*. This exercise will also help to develop your dexterity and speed up your reactions. You are forced to catch a ball one minute, a ring the next, and your fingers become nimble and flexible. You must also be able to shift quickly, from tossing one type of object to another.

Once you have practised the triple play well, you are ready for four rings. Juggle two rings with each hand. It is especially effective when four rings spin through the air.

You can also try tossing and catching five rings. Here, you pass the beginner's level and, with enough skill, earn the admiration and applause of your audience. You can find more detailed information on this quintuple juggling in the section: Juggling with Five Balls. Remember, though, that ring juggling always requires higher space.

In giving a performance of ring juggling, always stand sidewise to your audience. This way, the *surface* of the rings is in full view.

You can also learn triple juggling with rings in one hand.

Toss two rings up first, and then the third (taking it quickly from your other hand).

Another trick that will add to your performances is spinning a ring about your wrist or ankle. You can learn this easily, and those watching you will be all the more impressed with your skill.

To make one-handed juggling of balls or rings especially effective, try the following, using your other arm (with its free hand).

1. While two rings or balls are dancing up and down in one hand, stretch your other arm, where another ring is hanging, out to the side. A small swing will start this ring spinning. All you need is a little skill to keep this other ring moving lightly and easily.

2. Place one ring first on your right and then on your left wrist. Practise spinning this ring with your arms stretched out horizontally. Then put a ring on *both* your left and right arms, and make them spin together. Alternate, by spinning them in the opposite direction. Now put both rings on the same arm and make them spin together. Then try to get them turning in *opposite* directions.

There is no limit to the variations you can try! You probably know how to swing a large ring or hula hoop about your hips. Use this same motion to start your ring turning, and then keep it spinning.

You can juggle three rings or balls in the same fashion as

two. Here, of course, you will have no hands free, but a ring can spin just as well about an ankle! To practise, stand on one foot and bend your other leg backwards to form a right angle. Slip a ring over this ankle and give it a light push with your hand, to start it spinning. Try to keep it spinning by moving the bent portion of your leg. After a few tries, you should succeed. Then practise the same thing with your other leg.

Fig. 15. Here's a real show-stopper! Good co-ordination and a little practice are the answer.

You can juggle balls or rings while standing on one foot. Soon, this double motion of juggling three items with your hands while spinning a ring on your ankle will come easily to you. Be sure you have a friend with a camera nearby, to catch your picture in this impressive pose.

Here are some other variations you can try, with what you have learned so far:

(a) Spin a ring around each wrist and one ankle—three rings in all—at the same time (see picture).

(b) Spin two rings, one on a wrist and another on an ankle, while juggling two balls (Fig. 15).

(c) Using four rings, juggle two while spinning the other two around a wrist and an ankle.

(d) Using four balls, juggle two with each hand while spinning one ring around an ankle.

(e) Using five rings, juggle two with each hand and spin the fifth around an ankle.

You can invent further combinations, of course. Let your guests try their hand, (and foot!) at the simpler ones. This is a sure way to liven up any group you are entertaining.

JUGGLING WITH CLUBS

You must at some time have seen jugglers working with clubs. These clubs have to be the right shape to be suitable for tossing and catching. You can make them yourself, if you wish, just as you made your own rings.

First, take three round sticks of wood—about as thick as a broomstick—and about 16 in. long. You can find such sticks in any carpentry or wood-working shop. Or, if you have an old worn-out broom available, just saw off the handle to make the sticks. You can not use thinner sticks, however, since they do not lie as well in your hand. You will also need cardboard of medium thickness (like that used for shoe boxes) to make the bodies of your clubs.

The club's shape is that of a four-sided pyramid, with another four-sided pyramid sitting on it. (See Fig. 16.) This diagram shows the entire surface of the club, opened out flat. If you cut this out and folded it, you would have the body of the club.

On your cardboard, draw one full side, using the dimensions given. Now trace this side and you will have the full surface, without having to measure the angles or use a compass. If it doesn't come out quite right, ask your father or someone else to help you with it. Do not forget to draw in the edge flaps, for you will need these to glue the club together.

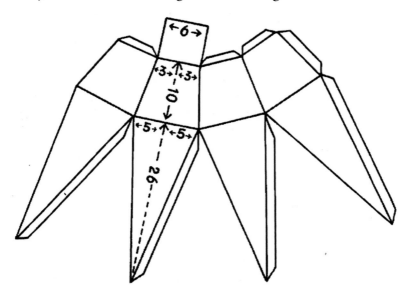

Fig. 16. This shows what a four-sided club looks like, opened out flat. You can make this yourself, out of heavy cardboard.

Now cut out the surface carefully, with sharp scissors, and bend all the edges to form your club. Glue together the sides of the cutoff upper section, first. Then glue down the square, on top of the flaps. When everything has dried thoroughly, take a stick and insert it so that it touches the middle of the square exactly. (You can get the exact point by drawing lines which join the corners of the square.) Next, fasten the stick to the square with glue and nails. The best way to do this is with a flat-headed nail, which you drive down through the cardboard into the stick.

Now you are ready to glue together the long ends of the club's body. Glue the lower ends of the cardboard to the stick and bind them. For binding, use a strong yarn and wind each strand right next to the other so that no bumps appear. To make your clubs more durable, cover all seams with cellophane tape. Your clubs are now ready to be used. Fig. 17 shows a completed club, with its short extended handle.

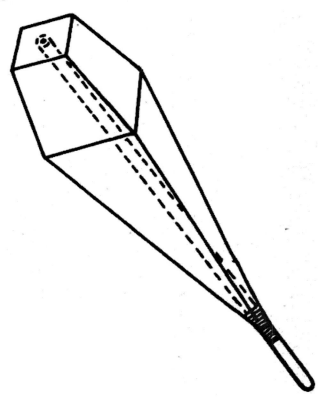

Fig. 17. Four-sided club, with short extended handle.

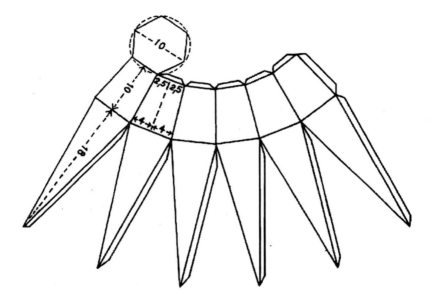

Fig. 18. Diagram of six-sided club, opened out flat.

When practising, it is a good idea to have a soft covering (a woollen blanket will do) on the floor. This way you prevent the club bodies from striking the floor too hard. You will have to expect a few unsuccessful tosses in the beginning! Besides this set of clubs, you will want to make a second set for performances later on.

To make your clubs as attractive as possible, cover their surfaces with bright luminous paper. Brilliant hues animate all juggling tricks.

Fig. 19 shows a six-sided club. To make it, draw a circle of the size you want. Without changing the compass setting, mark off lines on the circumference of the circle. The radius fits exactly six times into the circumference, making an equilateral hexagon. On one side of this hexagon draw a trapezoid with a long triangle extending downwards from its base. By drawing the same figure for each of the six sides in turn, you get a pattern for cutting which results this time in a six-sided club (Fig. 18).

After your clubs are completed, you can begin. Practise a turning toss, first, using one club. To do this, hold the handle of the club—remember, it is short—as comfortably as possible with the full surface of your hand (not just your fingertips). Your fingers should lie easily, and somewhat spread out, against the conical body of the club. You should also hold the lower end of the cardboard section of your club. In a good toss and catch, the hand grips the lower part of the club as well as the handle. Once you have the correct hold, throw the club into the air with a slight twist so that it drops back into your hand after making a complete turn. Practise this throw repeatedly. If you do not throw with enough force, the club will not make a complete turn and will be hard to catch. If you throw with too much force, however, the club will turn too quickly and its handle will not return to your hand.

At first, try only one rotation. The club can turn as many as three or four times in the air; it is just a question of whether you can catch it again by the handle. When you are practising, you will soon get used to the rhythm of the club's rotation. The club's center of gravity is just past the middle of the stick, so you will notice a definite swing back. If you have ever tried to spin a small hammer, you have noticed its tendency to swing back. There, the center of gravity is very far forward, however, so that the wooden handle of the hammer swings back into the palm of your hand very quickly, after a turn. Such an unbalanced club would not be suitable for juggling.

Start practising with two clubs at first, then use three, and so on. Soon, you will have learned a new juggling act. If a friend wants to try it, hand him your clubs. He will soon learn that it is not as easy as it looks! And he will admire your skill even more.

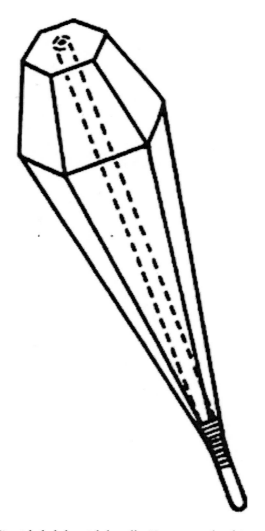

Fig. 19. Six-sided club, with handle. You can make this yourself by drawing a circle (the size you want) and marking off equal lines on its circumference. The radius should fit exactly six times into the circumference, making an equilateral hexagon.

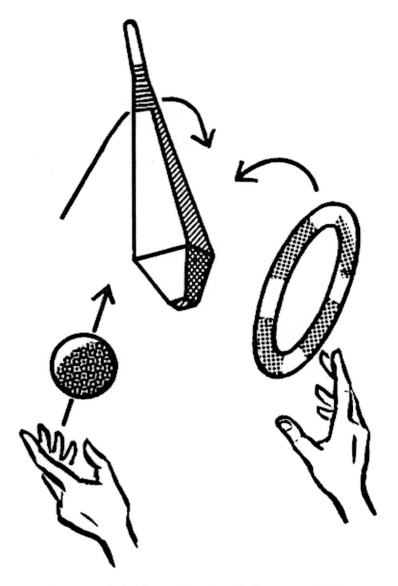

Fig. 20. A little of everything here: ball, ring, and club!

When you are ready, you can combine balls and rings with your club juggling. Then you can juggle three *different* objects in your hands. See Fig. 20. With this combination, you need only to concentrate on catching the *club*, for by now throwing and catching the ball and ring will be very easy. Once you have mastered the trick of getting the club to turn in the air, you can alternate by letting it turn twice while you are juggling.

397445LV00001B/29/P

LVOW12s141304081 4
Printed in the USA
CPSIA information can be obtained at www.ICGtesting.com

MAR 7 9 2015